Mary Anning:

The Girl Who Cracked Open the World

Written by Debora Pearson

Illustrated by Frances Castle

This edition of Mary Anning: The Girl Who Cracked Open the World is published by Pearson Education Inc. by arrangement with Pearson Education Limited. All rights reserved. Printed in Mexico.

Acknowledgments
The publisher would like to thank the following for their kind permission to reproduce their photographs: (Key: b-bottom; c-center; l-left; r-right; t-top) **Alamy Images:** MERVYN REES 10, Pictorial Press Ltd 20, The Natural History Museum 16, 21, 31; **Shutterstock.com:** abimages 7 (chisel), Bennyartist 7, Sergey Lavrentev 16 (fossils) All other images © Pearson Education

Every effort has been made to trace the copyright holders and we apologize in advance for any unintentional omissions. We would be pleased to insert the appropriate acknowledgment in any subsequent edition of this publication.

ISBN-13: 978-0-328-83292-7
ISBN-10: 0-328-83292-8

2 3 4 5 6 7 8 9 10 V0B4 19 18 17 16 15

"Mary! Mary!

Where are you going?"

Out of the cottage, away from her chores, and down
to the sea—that's where Mary was going. Over rocks
slippery with seaweed slime, near the crumbling cliffs of
England's south coast—that's where you'd find Mary.

It was a dangerous place, a wild, windy world. Falling
pebbles plink-plonked off her bonnet, but Mary didn't
care. There were fossils here, ancient fish teeth and curly
shells, and animal bones in the rock. "Curiosities" or
"curios," the treasure seekers called them. They were odd,
dainty things to look at and "ooh!" and "ahh!" over—and
Mary's family could sell as many as she could find.

But were those rock creatures alive at one time? When did they live? What did they do?

Did anyone think about this?

Shivering under her quilt at night, Mary thought of these things. Her feet were sore and her back ached from hours and hours hunched like a gull picking away at the rocks. But still she thought . . .

She wondered again as she closed her eyes. But the mystery in the rocks would have to wait. Mary was fast asleep.

One dark stormy day, Mary sat in her father's workshop, a cozy, dusty place. It was quiet too. No one was there except Mary and her father, the two fossil finders hard at work.

Her father chip-chipped away at rocks until the fossils appeared. Mary took the tiny pick that her father made for her and chip-chipped away bits of rock too. Everything Mary knew about fossils, she learned while working with her father.

When the storm ended, Mary grabbed her basket, hammer, and chisel. She ran out of the workshop and straight to the sea. Mary knew that after a storm was the best time to search for fossils. The wind and water broke the cliffs open, and fossils that had been buried were now exposed.

Mary picked through the rocks. Soon her fingers were numb from the cold. Her skirts were muddy and wet, but Mary didn't mind. She was happy there, looking for fossils and helping her father.

"What kind of girl spends her days like that?"

"Shouldn't Mary be indoors at school?"

The townspeople wondered and whispered these things whenever they saw Mary. Mary, they said, had always been different. Was it because she had been struck by lightning when she was a tiny, sickly baby?

There were three townspeople near Mary that day who were struck by lightning too. They didn't survive; only Mary did. And look at her now—curious, stubborn, and independent. Mary did whatever she wanted to do.

When Mary was eleven, her father died. Soon after that, she stepped into his dusty workshop. It looked the same, but something had changed. Sadness hung in the air, it lurked in the shadows, and Mary couldn't bear to be there.

She went down to the cliffs, noisy with seabirds and crashing waves, but it was no better there. Every fossil she found made her think of her father.

So Mary stayed away from her favorite places . . .

. . . until one day, after a storm, Mary was too curious to stay away any longer. She gathered her basket, hammer, and chisel and hurried down to the shore.

Her brother, Joseph, came along too. And when he found an enormous fossil, they forgot their troubles—at least for a while.

It was a skull almost as long as a horse! There was room in its mouth for hundreds of teeth! Mary stared at the eye sockets, great gaping holes, and pictured the eyes that once filled those spaces.

After digging and searching, and more digging and searching, Mary found the rest of the creature— its ribs, its backbone, everything. The skeleton was too long and heavy for Mary to move by herself. She needed the help of several people to haul everything all the way home.

They carried the bones, still encased in rock, into the dim, dusty workshop. Mary looked around, and then she picked up her tools. It was time to get to work.

Slowly, she chip-chipped the rock away. She cleaned and shined the bones. She studied them closely and saw how they fit together. When she was finished, she was certain that every bone was in the right place.

She stood back and stared.

What was this creature?

Some people said it was a monster. Mary thought it was simply magnificent.

The skeleton was sold and sent to a museum in the city of London. Scientists there couldn't wait to see it and name it. It was the first complete skeleton of this creature that anyone had ever found in the world.

This creature, the scientists believed, lived millions of years ago. They wanted to know more about Earth long ago, and the bones helped them do that. The men quickly forgot about the girl who found what they were looking at.

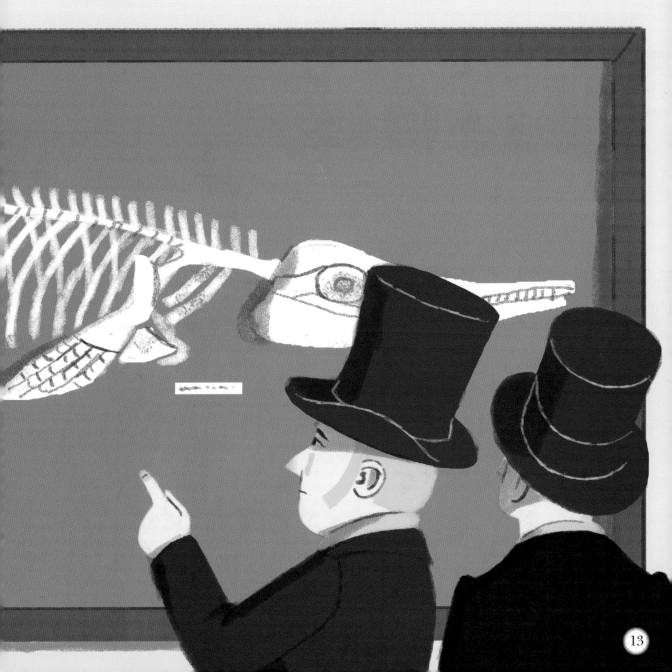

After much talking and arguing, the scientists named the creature. They called it "fish lizard" or "ichthyosaur."

The ichthyosaur was put on display so everyone could see it. When people asked, "Who found this creature?" sometimes Mary's name was mentioned, but most of the time no one talked about Mary. The men who studied the creature and named it were mentioned instead. They were scientists, they were experts. Mary was just a poor girl without much education who was lucky to find the creature. What did she know?

Mary knew plenty of things, and as the years passed by she learned more and more.

She cut open dead fish on her kitchen table so she could see how they looked inside. It was messy work, but Mary wanted to learn all that she could about fish. Maybe, she thought, this knowledge would help her understand fish that lived in the past.

She made detailed drawings of the fossils she found so she would remember them. She examined one fossil and compared it to another one. How were they similar? How were they different? Why? Mary wanted to know.

In the evening, before she went to bed, Mary wrote to scientists in other places. She asked them questions and then waited eagerly for the scientists to write back.

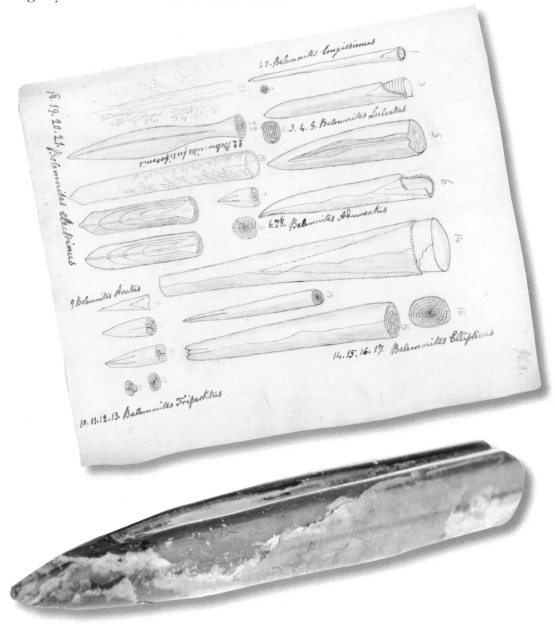

Mary was too poor to buy books, so whenever she could she borrowed other people's books about science. After she had read them, sometimes several times, she wrote down the important ideas.

Mary didn't know at the time, but she was doing the same work that all scientists did: she was asking questions, gathering information, and making drawings and notes of everything she studied.

When Henry De la Beche moved into town, people said to Mary, "You should meet Henry. He's very curious, just like you. And he also loves rocks and fossils."

After they met, Henry and Mary spent hours together talking about science. Henry's clothes were more expensive than Mary's. He didn't have to work for a living and sell fossils, the way Mary did. Henry and Mary were very different, but they didn't care. They were too busy becoming good friends and sharing ideas with each other.

Later, Henry helped Mary out when her family ran into trouble. Selling fossils was hard work, and sometimes the people who had money to buy curios weren't interested in Mary's things.

Henry came up with a plan to help Mary make money. First, he made a watercolor drawing of Mary's creatures as they would have looked in ancient times, when they were alive. His drawing was so real-looking that Mary felt as if she could step into the world he had created.

Henry took his drawing and arranged to have copies made. Other people liked the drawing as much as Mary did. The money that came from selling the copies was given to Mary and her family.

And something else good happened. People wanted to know more about the creatures in the drawings, and Mary's name was mentioned because she knew these animals from the inside out.

Mary's good friend Henry had helped her in ways she didn't expect.

Even before Henry helped her, Mary had made some very important discoveries. One day, as she stood by the cliffs, Mary spotted something new. It looked like a bone, maybe a skull. Was it another ichthyosaur?

Mary scraped away the rock . . . and found a creature she'd never seen before. It had a long neck, a tiny round head, and legs that were shaped like paddles. The creature looked so odd that some people thought it was made up and not real. Its skeleton, they said, must have been put together using the bones of a sea snake and an ichthyosaur.

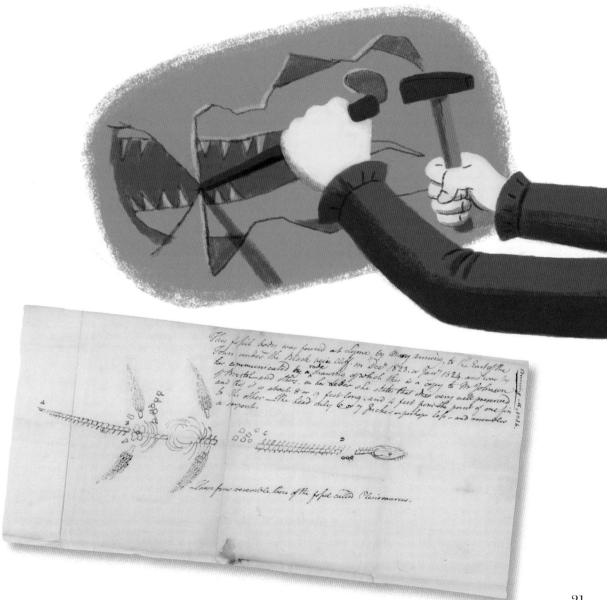

Mary was furious when she heard what people were saying about the skeleton she had discovered.

She knew fossils, and she knew what she had found. But some people weren't convinced until a group of scientists had spoken out. The scientists had found parts of creatures that looked the same as the skeleton Mary had found. Those creatures were called plesiosaurs.

The scientists knew fossils and they knew what they had found. Everyone believed them when they said Mary's plesiosaur was real and not made up.

This time, when people asked, "Who found this creature?" Mary's name was mentioned. She was becoming famous for the fossils she had found.

Scientists sent letters to her. They asked her questions about her discoveries, and then they waited eagerly for Mary to write back to them.

Now, when Mary hurried through town, visitors stopped and stared. They said to each other, "There goes the woman who found all those strange creatures. What do you think she is going to find next?"

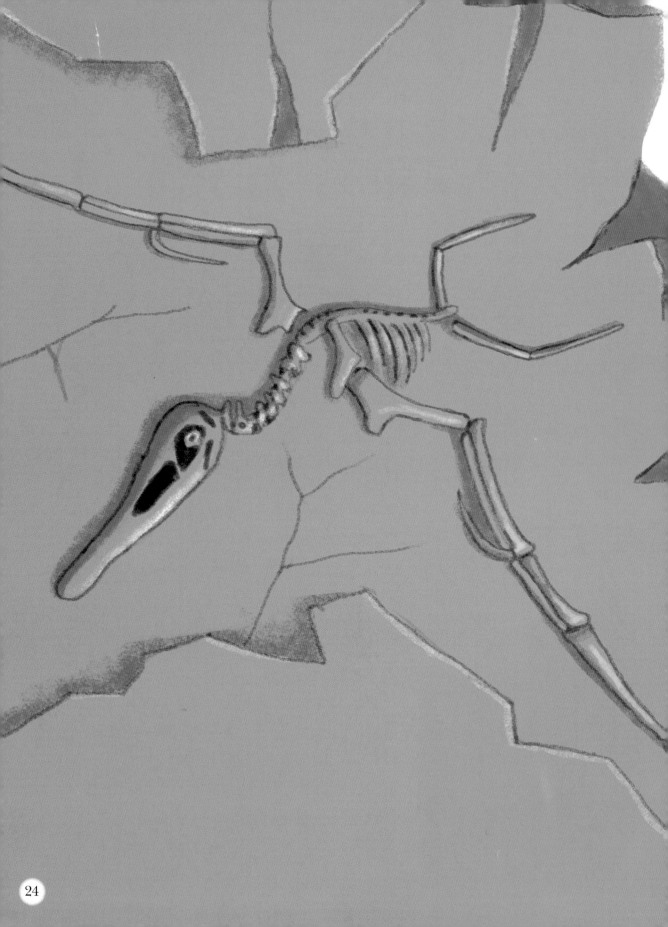

Mary was used to finding creatures that looked as if they swam in the water. But the creature she found next, still tucked in the cliff, was completely different.

It was shorter than Mary and—could it be?—it appeared to have wings and a beak. It must have been an ancient bird or a bat.

The creature turned out to be a "winged lizard" or "pterosaur," the first one ever found in England. Mary closed her eyes and tried to imagine it flapping overhead.

Slowly, slowly, bone by bone, Mary's fossil finds were adding to the knowledge that scientists had about Earth and its history. Her discoveries helped change what scientists chose to study from then on.

Some scientists were becoming experts in new kinds of science, such as geology, the study of rocks. Other scientists were fascinated by paleontology, the study of fossils and ancient life.

Meanwhile, day after day, year after year, Mary walked by the sea. Bone by bone, fossil by fossil, she learned more and more.

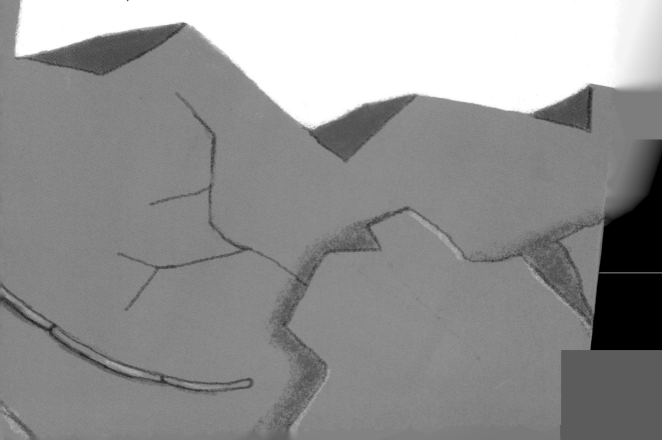

Inside Mary's fossil shop, visitors crowded around
[la]test discoveries. They came from all over Europe
[to m]eet her and ask her questions. After they left, Mary
[pack]aged up the fossils that collectors had bought. She
[built] a wooden frame for each one, and then gently
[laid] it inside and packed it with plaster.

[So]me of the fossils traveled by ship across the ocean
[to No]rth America, and other fossils traveled by wagon to
[Lond]on and places that were closer.

Along with the other creatures she discovered, Mary also found the fossils of ancient fish. When a scientist named Louis Agassiz learned that Mary had collected more than thirty kinds of fossil fish, he traveled all the way from Switzerland to meet Mary, look at her collection, and see the places where Mary had found the fish.

Louis was so grateful for her help that he named not only one, but two kinds of fossil fish after Mary.

Near the end of Mary's life, a scientist named Richard Owen used a new word, never heard before, to describe ancient creatures that lived on land. He called those creatures "terrible lizards" or "dinosaurs."

Mary's ichthyosaurs and plesiosaurs ruled the seas, and her pterosaurs ruled the skies. At the same time that those creatures lived, dinosaurs ruled the land. Many scientists were searching for dinosaur fossils. But not as many people were looking at the seas. Thanks to Mary, we have a more complete idea of what the world looked like during those times.

After Mary died, her good friend Henry talked about her at an important meeting in London. Since Henry first met Mary, he had become well-known for his work in geology. Now he was about to become the president of the Geological Society, and he wanted its members to remember Mary's important contributions to their work. During her life, Mary hadn't been able to become a member of the society because she was a woman. Only men were allowed to join.

Mary Anning spent her whole life in the place she loved best, near the sea and the crumbling cliffs with their fossils hidden deep inside. No one, not even Mary, expected that she would accomplish all that she did. No one thought that a poor girl without much education would find important fossils and learn so much about geology and paleontology. But that is exactly what happened.

Mary's love of fossils and her curious nature changed her life—and helped change the world of science too.

Glossary

chisel   A hand tool made of metal with a wooden handle that is used to cut or chip away rock and other hard materials

extinct   No longer existing or living

fossil   The remains or imprint of an animal or plant from long ago that is preserved in rock

geology   The study of the history of Earth, especially the rocks that it is made of

ichthyosaur   An extinct sea reptile with a long, pointed snout

paleontology   The study of ancient life on Earth and especially the study of fossils

plesiosaur   A large extinct sea reptile with a flattened body

pterosaur   An extinct flying reptile